Emotion & Cognition
in our Nervous System

Our nervous system receives information from our senses (sound, sight, smell, touch, taste); and helps us react to what is happening around us.

We are at our best when we can respond to challenges sensibly; adapting to changing conditions with an inner stability.

When we develop an awareness of emotions and thoughts, they can both work in balance. This helps us find the best course of action, even when faced with uncertain situations.

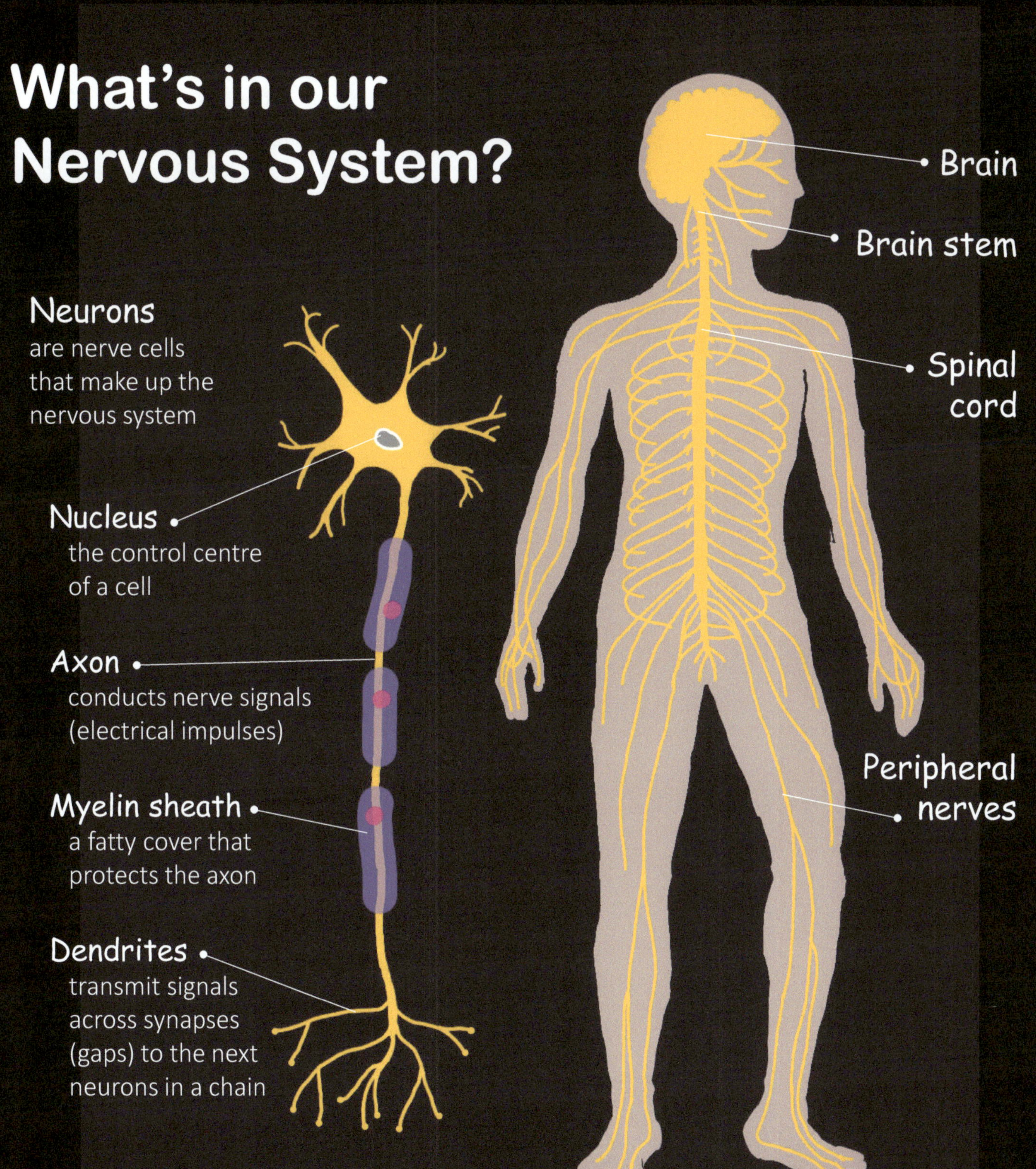

What's in our Nervous System?
Neurons
are nerve cells that make up the nervous system
Nucleus
the control centre of a cell
Axon
conducts nerve signals (electrical impulses)
Myelin sheath
a fatty cover that protects the axon
Dendrites
transmit signals across synapses (gaps) to the next neurons in a chain
Brain
Brain stem
Spinal cord
Peripheral nerves

那么……
不要让情绪压倒我们！
让它成为指导我们的工具
弄清楚它在做什么
然后加以疏导

So...
don't let emotions override us!
Use them as a tool to guide us

Figure out
what they're on about
Then navigate the flow!

孤独、疲惫；友善、亢奋

兴奋、平静、大胆或害羞

害怕失败还是勇敢尝试

知足、坚强；着急，错误

有时我们感到被背叛或愧疚

满心欢喜或忧心忡忡

我们可能会感到失落或有归属感

我们要不是意见不合，就是相处融洽

满意还是遗憾

雄心勃勃、受伤、绝望、伟大

……甚至可能是爱或恨……

Lonely, tired; friendly, wired
Excited, calm, bold or shy
Afraid to lose or dare to try
Contented, strong; anxious, wrong

Sometimes we feel betrayed or sorry
Full of joy or have a worry
We could feel lost or we belong
We're all at odds or get along

Satisfaction or regret
Ambitious, hurt, despairing, great
...maybe even love or hate...

有时我们很幸福

有时我们会悲伤

有时我们会感到愤怒

有时我感到庆幸

有时候我们厚颜无耻

有时候我们坏

也许我们觉得激动

也许我们感到生气

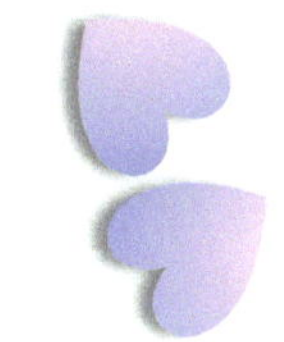

Sometime we are happy
Sometime we are sad
Sometimes we feel angry
Sometimes we feel glad

Sometimes we are cheeky
Sometimes we are bad
Maybe we feel geeky
Maybe we feel mad

I'm sorry... Please can you help?
This is how I'm feeling right now ...

情绪如潮，学会驾驭
根据不同情境，调整情绪反应
你不应该压抑自己的情绪
或失控地大喊大叫
情绪需要出口，但方式有别。
停下来，找出造成感觉的原因。
用最适当的言语
让他人理解是怎么一回事
倾听内心
追寻直觉
解释以便别人理解
或许，有人会伸出援手

We can't always control emotions
But we can learn their ebb and flow
And then we start to manage better
How and when they show

It's not that you should hold them in
Or that you scream or shout
Pause, and tell why you feel that way
Find the best words you can say
So others know what it's about

Know your heart, and check your gut
Explain so others understand
Maybe, you'll find a helping hand

每种情绪都有其价值

给我们传递重要的讯息

觉察并接纳大大小小的情绪

然后观其变化

有些情绪让我们感到难受或不愉快

或导致内心不舒服

它就像身体的警报器，

提醒我们可能面临危险

这些情绪在告诉我们：该停下来思考、快速行

动或寻求庇护。

倾听心声，智慧解决

（用头脑和心灵去解决问题）

All feelings are important
They tell us things we need to know
So big or small
Accept them all
Watch how they shrink or grow

Some feelings might be difficult
Or uncomfortable inside
They might warn us of a danger
Tell us: stop, or run, or hide

Learn to tune in to what they say
Use head and heart to be okay
(For both, together, save the day)

透过写作、音乐、艺术或沉浸在别人的作品
（故事、韵文或有趣的笑话）里，我们能将内
心深处的情感释放出来，感受到被理解的温暖，
进而提升心灵的平静
让我们重新找回身心舒畅
找回内心的健康与平衡
告别憋著屁的不适

We can let them out in writing
Or in music
Or in art
Or reading something someone wrote
(A story, rhyme, or funny joke)
That shows us that they understood
And that can help us to feel good

So that we feel alright again
And not ill inside our gut
(The way it feels uncomfortable
When we're holding in a fart)

我们可以以安全且有益的方式
照顾好自己的情绪
注意自己的情绪
不把它推开

We can take care of our emotions
In a safe and helpful way
Being attentive to our feelings
We don't push them away

因为情绪和放屁的事……

在于知道它来的时候

去哪里找到安全的空间

在一个好地方

轻轻地释放它

Because the thing about feelings and
    farting…

Is knowing, when they grow
Where to find a safe space
In a good place
And gently let them go

有人告诉我一件有趣的事——

她说情绪就像放屁

他们由内升起

那是错误的轨道！

不要把它逼回去——

你应该释放它

……否则有些东西可能会爆炸！

但是－不要释放得臭气熏天！

花点时间，停下来思考一下

Someone told me a funny thing-
She said feelings are like farts

They come bubbling up
From inside parts...
Don't force them back -
That's the wrong track!
You're meant to let them go
... or something might explode!

But – don't do it to make a stink!
Take a moment, pause and think...

有时我们很幸福

有时我们会悲伤

有时我们感到愤怒

有时我们感到庆幸

还有很多不一样的情绪

（有几种？你能全部说出来吗？）

每一个都可以如此强烈，令人恐惧

或有时小而安静

Sometimes we are happy
Sometimes we are sad
Sometimes we feel angry
Sometimes we feel glad

There's lots more different feelings
(How many? Can you name them all?)

Each can be so strong it's scary
Or sometimes quiet and small

This book belongs to

2023, ISBN 9798869505415 (Large print 8.5 x 8.5")
2023, ISBN 9798867609832 (Small format 6x6")
2023, Mini edition (4x4")
2024, ISBN 978-967-25547-4-5 (bi-lingual Chi-Eng 8.5 x 8.5")
eBooks available on Kindle and Google Books

www.EveVerne.com

Emotions are like… Farts

And we can manage them better

情緒就像⋯放屁

我們可以更好地管理它

Eve Verne 怡文

Translated by Dr Leong Yuen Yoong

翻譯者 梁圓融